W9-BTP-124

CHECKERBOARD BIOGRAPHY LIBRARY

U.S. PRESIDENTS

*The*
*United States Presidents*

# WARREN G. HARDING

ABDO Publishing Company

Heidi M.D. Elston

## visit us at
## www.abdopublishing.com

Published by ABDO Publishing Company, 8000 West 78th Street, Edina, Minnesota 55439.
Copyright © 2009 by Abdo Consulting Group, Inc. International copyrights reserved in all
countries. No part of this book may be reproduced in any form without written permission from the
publisher. The Checkerboard Library™ is a trademark and logo of ABDO Publishing Company.

Printed in the United States.

Cover Photo: Corbis
Interior Photos: American Political History p. 20; AP Images p. 19; Corbis pp. 5, 8, 10, 22;
      Getty Images pp. 11, 13, 23, 27, 28; iStockphoto p. 32; Library of Congress p. 18;
      National Archives p. 21; Ohio Historical Society pp. 12, 14–15, 21, 29; Picture History pp. 9,
      17, 25

Editor: Megan M. Gunderson
Art Direction & Cover Design: Neil Klinepier
Interior Design: Jaime Martens

### Library of Congress Cataloging-in-Publication Data

Elston, Heidi M. D., 1979-
  Warren G. Harding / Heidi M.D. Elston.
    p. cm. -- (The United States presidents)
  Includes bibliographical references and index.
  ISBN 978-1-60453-454-2
  1. Harding, Warren G. (Warren Gamaliel), 1865-1923--Juvenile literature. 2. Presidents--United
States--Biography--Juvenile literature. I. Title.
  E786.E45 2009
  973.91'4092--dc22
  [B]
                          2008035315

# CONTENTS

# WARREN G. HARDING

Warren G. Harding was the twenty-ninth president of the United States. He won the 1920 election by more than 7 million **popular votes**.

As a young man, Harding bought a struggling newspaper and made it a success. He later became a U.S. senator. As a senator, Harding did his best to help Americans. Yet, he wanted to reach more people. So in 1920, Harding ran for president of the United States.

**World War I** had recently ended. Many Americans were out of work and had little money. Harding promised to return the country to a simpler, easier time. He easily won the election.

President Harding was popular. But his **administration** suffered through **scandals**. Still, Harding remained honest and worked hard for the people.

After less than three years as president, Harding died. He was the sixth U.S. president to die in office. After Harding's death, **Republican** presidents continued to follow his policies through the 1920s.

# TIMELINE

**1865** - On November 2, Warren Gamaliel Harding was born in Corsica, Ohio.

**1882** - Harding graduated from Ohio Central College in Iberia, Ohio.

**1891** - On July 8, Harding married Florence Kling DeWolfe.

**1898** - Harding won election to the Ohio state senate.

**1901** - Harding was reelected to the Ohio senate.

**1902** - Harding was elected lieutenant governor of Ohio.

**1912** - At the Republican National Convention, Harding announced President William Taft's nomination for reelection.

**1914** - Harding won election to the U.S. Senate.

**1917** - The United States entered World War I.

**1918** - The Allies won World War I.

**1919** - The Eighteenth Amendment was approved on January 29. It banned the manufacture and sale of alcohol; in October, Congress adopted the Volstead Act to enforce the amendment.

**1920** - On August 26, the Nineteenth Amendment was added to the U.S. Constitution. This gave all women the right to vote; Harding campaigned for president with the slogan "Back to Normalcy"; on November 2, Harding won the election.

**1921** - Harding was inaugurated the twenty-ninth U.S. president on March 4.

**1923** - Harding went on a speaking tour across the nation; on August 2, President Warren G. Harding died.

# DID YOU KNOW?

Warren G. Harding was the first president to ride in an automobile to and from his inauguration.

Harding was the first president to have a radio in the White House. And, he was the first president to give a speech over the radio.

President Harding dedicated the Lincoln Memorial on May 30, 1922. The Lincoln Memorial honors the sixteenth U.S. president, Abraham Lincoln. It is located in Washington, D.C.

Harding wore size 14 shoes! Of all U.S. presidents, Harding's feet were the largest.

Harding's dog Laddie Boy had a birthday party at the White House. A frosted cake made from dog biscuits was served.

# GROWING UP IN OHIO

Warren Gamaliel Harding was born on November 2, 1865, in Corsica, Ohio. Corsica is now called Blooming Grove. Warren's parents were George Tryon and Phoebe Dickerson Harding.

George supported his family by farming. He was also a country doctor and a trader. Phoebe was a **midwife**. Still, the Harding family was poor. Warren was the first of eight children. Growing up, he spent much of his time doing chores. These included cutting down trees, chopping wood, and planting and harvesting crops. Eventually, Warren's father became part owner of a weekly newspaper.

*George and Phoebe Harding*

## FAST FACTS

**BORN** - November 2, 1865
**WIFE** - Florence Kling DeWolfe (1860–1924)
**CHILDREN** - None
**POLITICAL PARTY** - Republican
**AGE AT INAUGURATION** - 55
**YEARS SERVED** - 1921–1923
**VICE PRESIDENT** - Calvin Coolidge
**DIED** - August 2, 1923, age 57

*Warren's birthplace*

It was called the *Caledonia Argus*. Warren helped any way he could. He soon learned to set **type**. Warren discovered he liked the newspaper business.

Warren attended a one-room school in Caledonia, Ohio. When he was 14, he entered Ohio Central College in Iberia, Ohio. There, Warren was popular. He edited the yearbook and entered speaking contests. Also, he played the alto horn. Warren graduated in 1882.

# FIRST JOBS

*Harding later said teaching was "the hardest job I ever had."*

After graduation, Harding moved to Marion, Ohio. His family had moved there while he was in school. In Marion, Harding managed the Marion Citizens' Cornet Band. He also played sports such as baseball.

During this time, Harding held many jobs. He taught school for one term. Harding also studied law. Then, he tried selling **insurance**.

Harding did not like any of these jobs. Then he remembered how much he had enjoyed the newspaper business. When he was 19, Harding became a reporter for the *Mirror*.

The *Mirror* was a **Democratic** weekly newspaper in Marion. However, Harding was already establishing himself as a loyal **Republican**.

During the 1884 presidential campaign, Harding supported Republican candidate James G. Blaine. He even wore a Blaine campaign hat to work. This upset the newspaper owners, so they fired Harding.

*Harding* (left) *remained a fan of baseball. While president, he entertained professional baseball player Babe Ruth* (right) *at the White House.*

# THE *MARION STAR*

In just a few weeks, Harding moved on to a different newspaper. The *Marion Star* was for sale for $300. Harding and two friends bought it. Now, Harding was a newspaper publisher!

*Harding working at the Marion Star. He is the first newspaper publisher to become a U.S. president.*

Most people believed Harding was foolish to buy the *Marion Star*. Its equipment badly needed repair. The newspaper did not have enough advertising money coming in. And, each **subscription** brought in only ten cents a week.

To help the newspaper succeed, Harding worked day and night. He operated the equipment, wrote articles, and sold advertising space.

Harding got help after he met Florence Kling DeWolfe. Florence had been born in Marion in 1860. The two fell in love and married on July 8, 1891. They had no children together.

Mrs. Harding began working at the *Marion Star*. Harding trusted his wife's good business sense. Slowly, she took over managing the newspaper. Mrs. Harding's hard work made it a success.

*Harding nicknamed his wife "Duchess."*

# ENTERING POLITICS

Now, Harding had more time for other interests. He wanted to make his community and state a better place to live. So, Harding entered politics. He went to town meetings and gave speeches. People liked his ideas. Harding soon made a name for himself as a skillful speaker.

Harding was elected to the Ohio state senate in 1898. There, he became one of the most popular senators. Harding was friendly. And, he helped keep peace within the **Republican** Party. Harding was reelected in 1901. He then became a party leader.

In 1902, Harding was elected lieutenant governor of Ohio. Harding ran for governor of Ohio in 1910. But he lost the election. Harding's political career seemed over.

Then in 1912, Harding gave an important speech at the **Republican National Convention**. There, he announced President William Taft's nomination for reelection. Harding impressed Republican Party leaders with his speaking ability.

*The Hardings built their Marion, Ohio, home in 1891.  Harding conducted his 1920 presidential campaign from this home's large porch.*

# SENATOR HARDING

In 1914, Harding ran for the U.S. Senate. He easily won the election. As a senator, Harding never introduced any major bills. But, he was well liked and popular.

During this time, many countries were fighting **World War I**. President Woodrow Wilson called a special meeting of Congress on April 2, 1917. He wanted the United States to enter the war and help the **Allies** win.

Eighty-two senators voted to go to war. Just six senators voted no. So, the United States went to war. In November 1918, the Allies won. On June 28, 1919, the Treaty of Versailles was signed in France. This officially declared peace between Germany and the Allies.

Following the war, President Wilson asked Congress to officially approve the Treaty of Versailles. But, Harding and many other **Republicans** strongly opposed him. They did not like the **League of Nations** agreement included in the treaty. The Senate defeated the treaty on November 19, 1919. The United States made a separate peace agreement with Germany in 1921.

*Harding served in the U.S. Senate for six years.*

# PROHIBITION

As a senator, Harding voted for two **amendments** to the U.S. **Constitution**. The Eighteenth Amendment stopped the manufacture and sale of alcohol in America. This was also known as the Prohibition Amendment. It was officially approved on January 29, 1919.

*U.S. officials destroying alcohol*

In October, Congress adopted the Volstead Act. This act provided for the enforcement of the Eighteenth Amendment. Still, enforcement varied. It was weaker in cities than in rural areas. This is because people in large cities strongly opposed Prohibition.

Prohibition ended the legal sale of alcohol in the United States. But people did not stop drinking it. Illegal sales of alcohol rose. And a new kind of criminal emerged. Bootleggers illegally supplied alcohol. Al Capone is one of the most famous bootleggers in U.S. history.

*Al Capone made about $60 million a year bootlegging.*

# WOMEN'S RIGHT TO VOTE

Senator Harding also voted for the Nineteenth **Amendment**. It gave women in all states the right to vote. The Nineteenth Amendment became part of the U.S. **Constitution** on August 26, 1920.

*The movement toward giving women the right to vote in all elections began in the early 1800s. Key leaders in this movement were Elizabeth Cady Stanton and Susan B. Anthony.*

Similar **amendments** had been introduced in Congress in 1878 and 1914. But, both proposals had been defeated.

Wyoming had been the first state to allow women the right to vote. It had become a state in 1890 with a **constitution** allowing for this privilege. By 1918, women had equal voting rights with men in 15 states.

People kept fighting for equal women's voting rights throughout the country. The Nineteenth Amendment was an important victory.

*Because of the Nineteenth Amendment (right),* Mrs. Harding (above) *was the first First Lady able to vote for her husband.*

# THE 1920 ELECTION

In 1920, Harding wanted to run for senator again. But that year, the **Republican** Party couldn't agree on a choice for president. Some Republican leaders began mentioning Harding as a possible candidate.

Later that year, Republican delegates nominated Harding for president. They chose Massachusetts governor Calvin Coolidge as his **running mate**. The **Democrats** chose Ohio governor James M. Cox to run for president. Franklin D. Roosevelt was nominated for vice president.

At this time, the U.S. **economy** was suffering. Businesses were failing, and people were losing their jobs. Americans blamed President Wilson and his fellow Democrats.

Harding promised to make the country better. He campaigned on the **slogan** "Back to Normalcy." On November 2, Harding won the election! He received more than 16 million **popular votes**. Cox won fewer than 10 million. Harding was the first president for whom all women could vote.

UNDER
The 19th
Amendment
I CAST MY
FIRST VOTE
Nov. 2nd, 1920

Harding
Coolidge

The Straight
Republican
Ticket

Lancaster, Pa.

*Calvin Coolidge* (left) *with Harding*

# PRESIDENT HARDING

On March 4, 1921, Harding was **inaugurated** the twenty-ninth U.S. president. He wanted to return the country to normalcy. So, Harding got right to work on keeping this campaign promise.

To help the U.S. **economy**, President Harding supported new laws. He allowed U.S. businesses to produce more goods. He also lowered taxes on goods made in America. But he raised taxes on products from other countries. The Fordney-McCumber Act of 1922 raised **tariffs** to the highest in history! And Harding slowed **immigration**.

Harding also had success in foreign affairs. He called for the Washington Conference on Limitation of Naval Armaments. There, leaders arranged treaties that limited the naval strengths of world powers.

President Harding also took a stand on labor. At the time, the nation's large steel companies had 12-hour workdays. Harding convinced them to shorten this.

# PRESIDENT HARDING'S CABINET

## MARCH 4, 1921–AUGUST 2, 1923

- **STATE** – Charles Evans Hughes
- **TREASURY** – Andrew W. Mellon
- **WAR** – John Wingate Weeks
- **NAVY** – Edwin Denby
- **ATTORNEY GENERAL** – Harry Micajah Daugherty

- **INTERIOR** – Albert Bacon Fall
  Hubert Work (from March 5, 1923)
- **AGRICULTURE** – Henry Cantwell Wallace
- **COMMERCE** – Herbert Hoover
- **LABOR** – James John Davis

*President Harding* (seated, third from right), *Vice President Coolidge*
(seated, second from right), *and cabinet members*

# TEAPOT DOME SCANDAL

President Harding was working hard. The American people had faith in him. But, there were problems within his **administration**. Congress uncovered crimes in the Justice Department and the Veterans Bureau. And some members of Harding's **cabinet** were dishonest.

Albert B. Fall was President Harding's secretary of the interior. He was in charge of America's natural resources. Fall led the Harding administration into one of the greatest **scandals** in U.S. history. It is called the Teapot Dome scandal.

Teapot Dome was a piece of government land in Wyoming. Fall secretly allowed only Harry F. Sinclair of the Mammoth Oil Company to drill on this land. In return, Fall received bribes. Fall later went to jail for his part in the scandal.

## SUPREME COURT APPOINTMENTS

WILLIAM TAFT - 1921
GEORGE SUTHERLAND - 1922
PIERCE BUTLER - 1923
EDWARD T. SANFORD - 1923

26

*Albert B. Fall (left) with Harry F. Sinclair*

# SPEAKING TOUR

Meanwhile, the **Republicans** had lost many seats in Congress during the 1922 elections. President Harding was deeply upset. He wanted to rebuild trust in his **administration**. So in 1923, he decided to take a speaking tour to talk to Americans. The trip would take him across the country, including Alaska.

While in Seattle, Washington, President Harding fell ill. He then traveled to California. In San Francisco on August 2, 1923, President Warren G. Harding died. Then, Vice President Coolidge became president.

Harding was buried in Marion. Florence Harding died in Marion the next year. She was buried next to her husband.

*President and Mrs. Harding traveled together across the country. Harding was the first president to visit Alaska and Canada while in office.*

*In Marion, a group of citizens raised money for Harding's tomb.*

Warren G. Harding was a popular president. Sadly, his presidency is remembered for the **scandals** that tarnished his **cabinet**. Harding desired to be America's "best-loved" president. He wanted to restore the war-weary country to a time of normalcy. Harding worked hard to achieve this goal and be a good leader.

# OFFICE OF THE PRESIDENT

## BRANCHES OF GOVERNMENT

The U.S. government is divided into three branches. They are the executive, legislative, and judicial branches. This division is called a separation of powers. Each branch has some power over the others. This is called a system of checks and balances.

### EXECUTIVE BRANCH

The executive branch enforces laws. It is made up of the president, the vice president, and the president's cabinet. The president represents the United States around the world. He or she oversees relations with other countries and signs treaties. The president signs bills into law and appoints officials and federal judges. He or she also leads the military and manages government workers.

### LEGISLATIVE BRANCH

The legislative branch makes laws, maintains the military, and regulates trade. It also has the power to declare war. This branch consists of the Senate and the House of Representatives. Together, these two houses make up Congress. Each state has two senators. A state's population determines the number of representatives it has.

### JUDICIAL BRANCH

The judicial branch interprets laws. It consists of district courts, courts of appeals, and the Supreme Court. District courts try cases. If a person disagrees with a trial's outcome, he or she may appeal. If the courts of appeals support the ruling, a person may appeal to the Supreme Court. The Supreme Court also makes sure that laws follow the U.S. Constitution.

## QUALIFICATIONS FOR OFFICE

To be president, a person must meet three requirements. A candidate must be at least 35 years old and a natural-born U.S. citizen. He or she must also have lived in the United States for at least 14 years.

## ELECTORAL COLLEGE

The U.S. presidential election is an indirect election. Voters from each state choose electors to represent them in the Electoral College. The number of electors from each state is based on population. Each elector has one electoral vote. Electors are pledged to cast their vote for the candidate who receives the highest number of popular votes in their state. A candidate must receive the majority of Electoral College votes to win.

## TERM OF OFFICE

Each president may be elected to two four-year terms. Sometimes, a president may only be elected once. This happens if he or she served more than two years of the previous president's term.

The presidential election is held on the Tuesday after the first Monday in November. The president is sworn in on January 20 of the following year. At that time, he or she takes the oath of office:

I do solemnly swear (or affirm) that I will faithfully execute the office of President of the United States, and will to the best of my ability, preserve, protect and defend the Constitution of the United States.

# LINE OF SUCCESSION

The Presidential Succession Act of 1947 defines who becomes president if the president cannot serve. The vice president is first in the line of succession. Next are the Speaker of the House and the President Pro Tempore of the Senate. If none of these individuals is able to serve, the office falls to the president's cabinet members. They would take office in the order in which each department was created:

| Secretary of State |
| --- |
| Secretary of the Treasury |
| Secretary of Defense |
| Attorney General |
| Secretary of the Interior |
| Secretary of Agriculture |
| Secretary of Commerce |
| Secretary of Labor |
| Secretary of Health and Human Services |
| Secretary of Housing and Urban Development |
| Secretary of Transportation |
| Secretary of Energy |
| Secretary of Education |
| Secretary of Veterans Affairs |
| Secretary of Homeland Security |

# Benefits

• While in office, the president receives a salary of $400,000 each year. He or she lives in the White House and has 24-hour Secret Service protection.

• The president may travel on a Boeing 747 jet called Air Force One. The airplane can accommodate 70 passengers. It has kitchens, a dining room, sleeping areas, and a conference room. It also has fully equipped offices with the latest communications systems. Air Force One can fly halfway around the world before needing to refuel. It can even refuel in flight!

• If the president wishes to travel by car, he or she uses Cadillac One. Cadillac One is a Cadillac Deville. It has been modified with heavy armor and communications systems. The president takes Cadillac One along when visiting other countries if secure transportation will be needed.

• The president also travels on a helicopter called Marine One. Like the presidential car, Marine One accompanies the president when traveling abroad if necessary.

• Sometimes, the president needs to get away and relax with family and friends. Camp David is the official presidential retreat. It is located in the cool, wooded mountains in Maryland. The U.S. Navy maintains the retreat, and the U.S. Marine Corps keeps it secure. The camp offers swimming, tennis, golf, and hiking.

• When the president leaves office, he or she receives Secret Service protection for ten more years. He or she also receives a yearly pension of $191,300 and funding for office space, supplies, and staff.

# PRESIDENTS AND THEIR TERMS

| PRESIDENT | PARTY | TOOK OFFICE | LEFT OFFICE | TERMS SERVED | VICE PRESIDENT |
|-----------|-------|-------------|-------------|--------------|----------------|
| George Washington | None | April 30, 1789 | March 4, 1797 | Two | John Adams |
| John Adams | Federalist | March 4, 1797 | March 4, 1801 | One | Thomas Jefferson |
| Thomas Jefferson | Democratic-Republican | March 4, 1801 | March 4, 1809 | Two | Aaron Burr, George Clinton |
| James Madison | Democratic-Republican | March 4, 1809 | March 4, 1817 | Two | George Clinton, Elbridge Gerry |
| James Monroe | Democratic-Republican | March 4, 1817 | March 4, 1825 | Two | Daniel D. Tompkins |
| John Quincy Adams | Democratic-Republican | March 4, 1825 | March 4, 1829 | One | John C. Calhoun |
| Andrew Jackson | Democrat | March 4, 1829 | March 4, 1837 | Two | John C. Calhoun, Martin Van Buren |
| Martin Van Buren | Democrat | March 4, 1837 | March 4, 1841 | One | Richard M. Johnson |
| William H. Harrison | Whig | March 4, 1841 | April 4, 1841 | Died During First Term | John Tyler |
| John Tyler | Whig | April 6, 1841 | March 4, 1845 | Completed Harrison's Term | Office Vacant |
| James K. Polk | Democrat | March 4, 1845 | March 4, 1849 | One | George M. Dallas |
| Zachary Taylor | Whig | March 5, 1849 | July 9, 1850 | Died During First Term | Millard Fillmore |

| PRESIDENT | PARTY | TOOK OFFICE | LEFT OFFICE | TERMS SERVED | VICE PRESIDENT |
|---|---|---|---|---|---|
| Millard Fillmore | Whig | July 10, 1850 | March 4, 1853 | Completed Taylor's Term | Office Vacant |
| Franklin Pierce | Democrat | March 4, 1853 | March 4, 1857 | One | William R.D. King |
| James Buchanan | Democrat | March 4, 1857 | March 4, 1861 | One | John C. Breckinridge |
| Abraham Lincoln | Republican | March 4, 1861 | April 15, 1865 | Served One Term, Died During Second Term | Hannibal Hamlin, Andrew Johnson |
| Andrew Johnson | Democrat | April 15, 1865 | March 4, 1869 | Completed Lincoln's Second Term | Office Vacant |
| Ulysses S. Grant | Republican | March 4, 1869 | March 4, 1877 | Two | Schuyler Colfax, Henry Wilson |
| Rutherford B. Hayes | Republican | March 3, 1877 | March 4, 1881 | One | William A. Wheeler |
| James A. Garfield | Republican | March 4, 1881 | September 19, 1881 | Died During First Term | Chester Arthur |
| Chester Arthur | Republican | September 20, 1881 | March 4, 1885 | Completed Garfield's Term | Office Vacant |
| Grover Cleveland | Democrat | March 4, 1885 | March 4, 1889 | One | Thomas A. Hendricks |
| Benjamin Harrison | Republican | March 4, 1889 | March 4, 1893 | One | Levi P. Morton |
| Grover Cleveland | Democrat | March 4, 1893 | March 4, 1897 | One | Adlai E. Stevenson |
| William McKinley | Republican | March 4, 1897 | September 14, 1901 | Served One Term, Died During Second Term | Garret A. Hobart, Theodore Roosevelt |

| PRESIDENT | PARTY | TOOK OFFICE | LEFT OFFICE | TERMS SERVED | VICE PRESIDENT |
|---|---|---|---|---|---|
| Theodore Roosevelt | Republican | September 14, 1901 | March 4, 1909 | Completed McKinley's Second Term, Served One Term | Office Vacant, Charles Fairbanks |
| William Taft | Republican | March 4, 1909 | March 4, 1913 | One | James S. Sherman |
| Woodrow Wilson | Democrat | March 4, 1913 | March 4, 1921 | Two | Thomas R. Marshall |
| Warren G. Harding | Republican | March 4, 1921 | August 2, 1923 | Died During First Term | Calvin Coolidge |
| Calvin Coolidge | Republican | August 3, 1923 | March 4, 1929 | Completed Harding's Term, Served One Term | Office Vacant, Charles Dawes |
| Herbert Hoover | Republican | March 4, 1929 | March 4, 1933 | One | Charles Curtis |
| Franklin D. Roosevelt | Democrat | March 4, 1933 | April 12, 1945 | Served Three Terms, Died During Fourth Term | John Nance Garner, Henry A. Wallace, Harry S. Truman |
| Harry S. Truman | Democrat | April 12, 1945 | January 20, 1953 | Completed Roosevelt's Fourth Term, Served One Term | Office Vacant, Alben Barkley |
| Dwight D. Eisenhower | Republican | January 20, 1953 | January 20, 1961 | Two | Richard Nixon |
| John F. Kennedy | Democrat | January 20, 1961 | November 22, 1963 | Died During First Term | Lyndon B. Johnson |
| Lyndon B. Johnson | Democrat | November 22, 1963 | January 20, 1969 | Completed Kennedy's Term, Served One Term | Office Vacant, Hubert H. Humphrey |
| Richard Nixon | Republican | January 20, 1969 | August 9, 1974 | Completed First Term, Resigned During Second Term | Spiro T. Agnew, Gerald Ford |

| PRESIDENT | PARTY | TOOK OFFICE | LEFT OFFICE | TERMS SERVED | VICE PRESIDENT |
|---|---|---|---|---|---|
| Gerald Ford | Republican | August 9, 1974 | January 20, 1977 | Completed Nixon's Second Term | Nelson A. Rockefeller |
| Jimmy Carter | Democrat | January 20, 1977 | January 20, 1981 | One | Walter Mondale |
| Ronald Reagan | Republican | January 20, 1981 | January 20, 1989 | Two | George H.W. Bush |
| George H.W. Bush | Republican | January 20, 1989 | January 20, 1993 | One | Dan Quayle |
| Bill Clinton | Democrat | January 20, 1993 | January 20, 2001 | Two | Al Gore |
| George W. Bush | Republican | January 20, 2001 | January 20, 2009 | Two | Dick Cheney |
| Barack Obama | Democrat | January 20, 2009 | | | Joe Biden |

*"We must have a citizenship less concerned about what the government can do for it and more anxious about what it can do for the nation." Warren G. Harding*

# WRITE TO THE PRESIDENT

You may write to the president at:

**The White House
1600 Pennsylvania Avenue NW
Washington, DC 20500**

You may e-mail the president at:
**comments@whitehouse.gov**

# GLOSSARY

**administration** - the people who manage a presidential government.

**allies** - people, groups, or nations united for some special purpose. During World War I Great Britain, France, Russia, Italy, and Japan were called the Allies.

**amendment** - a change to a country's constitution.

**cabinet** - a group of advisers chosen by the president to lead government departments.

**constitution** - the laws that govern a country or a state. The U.S. Constitution is the laws that govern the United States.

**Democrat** - a member of the Democratic political party. Democrats believe in social change and strong government.

**economy** - the way a nation uses its money, goods, and natural resources.

**immigration** - entry into another country to live. A person who immigrates is called an immigrant.

**inaugurate** (ih-NAW-gyuh-rayt) - to swear into a political office.

**insurance** - a contract that helps people pay their bills if they are sick or hurt. People with insurance pay money each month to keep the contract.

**League of Nations** - an international association created to maintain peace among the nations of the world.

**midwife** - a person who assists women in childbirth.

**popular vote** - the vote of the entire body of people with the right to vote.

**Republican** - a member of the Republican political party. Republicans are conservative and believe in small government.

**Republican National Convention** - a national meeting held every four years during which the Republican Party chooses its candidates for president and vice president.

**running mate** - a candidate running for a lower-rank position on an election ticket, especially the candidate for vice president.

**scandal** - an action that shocks people and disgraces those connected with it.

**slogan** - a word or a phrase used to express a position, a stand, or a goal.

**subscription** - a purchase by prepayment for a certain number of issues of a publication, such as a newspaper or a magazine.

**tariff** - the taxes a government puts on imported or exported goods.

**type** - a piece of metal or wood bearing on the upper surface a raised letter, number, or other figure for use in printing.

**World War I** - from 1914 to 1918, fought in Europe. Great Britain, France, Russia, the United States, and their allies were on one side. Germany, Austria-Hungary, and their allies were on the other side.

# WEB SITES

To learn more about Warren G. Harding, visit ABDO Publishing Company on the World Wide Web at **www.abdopublishing.com**. Web sites about Warren G. Harding are featured on our Book Links page. These links are routinely monitored and updated to provide the most current information available.

# INDEX